GW00382525

From EXMOUTH *... With Love*

GEORGE PRIDMORE

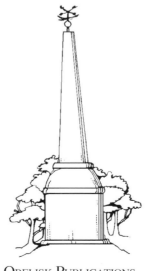

OBELISK PUBLICATIONS

ALSO BY THE AUTHOR:

Wish You Were Here ... at Exmouth

SOME OTHER TITLES OF INTEREST FROM OBELISK PUBLICATIONS:

Exmouth and Surrounding Area:

The Lost City of Exeter, Chips Barber
Adventure Through Red Devon, Raymond B. Cattell
The Great Little Exeter Book, Chips Barber
Talking About Topsham, Sara Vernon
Exeter in Colour, Chips Barber
The Ghosts of Exeter, Sally & Chips Barber
ExtraOrdinary Exmouth, Harry Pascoe
Dawlish and Dawlish Warren, Chips Barber
Ten Family Walks in East Devon, Sally & Chips Barber
Ian Jubb's *Exeter Collection*

Devon Area

Under Sail Through South Devon & Dartmoor, R. B. Cattell
The Great Walks of Dartmoor, Terry Bound
Diary of a Devonshire Walker, Chips Barber
The Great Little Dartmoor Book, Chips Barber
Albert Labbett's *Crediton Collection, parts I and II*
TV and Films Made in Devon, Chips Barber & David FitzGerald
Dartmoor in Colour, Chips Barber
Dark & Dastardly Dartmoor, Sally & Chips Barber
Tales of the Unexplained in Devon, Judy Chard
Haunted Happenings in Devon, Judy Chard
Ten Family Walks on Dartmoor, Sally & Chips Barber
The A to Z of Dartmoor Tors, Terry Bound
Weird & Wonderful Dartmoor, Sally & Chips Barber
The Templer Way, Derek Beavis
Ghastly and Ghostly Devon, Sally & Chips Barber
More...Cobblestones, Cottages and Castles, David Young

If you would like further details of currently available titles, please send an s.a.e. to the address given below or telephone (0392) 68556.

This book is dedicated to all my grandchildren.

First published in 1993 by
Obelisk Publications, 2 Church Hill, Pinhoe, Exeter, Devon
Designed by Chips and Sally Barber
Typeset by Sally Barber
Printed in Great Britain by
Ashley House, Marsh Barton, Exeter, Devon

from **EXMOUTH**... *With Love*

This book is a sequel to "Wish You Were Here ... at Exmouth". Like its predecessor it features postcards sent from, and connected with, the seaside resort of Exmouth.

For many years the sending of postcards has been a recognised tradition while on holiday but this collection also includes cards used for other purposes.

For example, simply to keep in touch; to convey birthday, Christmas or New Year greetings; for business purposes; as a souvenir of a special event; and even one written just to tell someone that it is snowing – yes, in Exmouth!

Postcards also have their place in recording social history. While the pictures illustrate how the appearance of places and people may have altered, the messages often demonstrate changes in attitudes and interests. I hope you enjoy this nostalgic journey into Exmouth of yesteryear.

GREETINGS FROM EXMOUTH

The place where many postcards from Exmouth began their journey – the town's Post Office as it was from 1878 to 1911. These premises in The Parade now house the Oasis Shopping Centre.

THE STRAND, EXMOUTH.

In earlier times the Post Office was situated in The Strand, on the site now occupied by Lloyds Bank. This postcard dates from the days before some of the properties along from the bank were destroyed by a bomb dropped during an air-raid in 1943. Note that the Strand Gardens were enclosed by iron railings.

Exmouth from the Warren

Postmarked 1915, this card shows the pleasure boat *Duchess of Devonshire* off the sea-front. The panoramic view includes several local landmarks like the Beacon, Gentlemen's Club (now Elizabeth Hall), Imperial Hotel, Clock Tower and Holy Trinity Church, with the spire of Tower Street Methodist Church just visible on the left. The card was sold at John Land's Empire Stores on the corner of Rolle Street and High Street. The picture was taken from The Warren at a time when the gap between it and Exmouth was about half what it is today!

A view dating from pre-Second World War days showing Dalwish Warren when it was occupied by several bungalows and chalets used as holiday or weekend homes. Some of the properties were built on stilts.

This 1913 card shows the sea-front bustling with activity – Chudley's ice-cream cart; drivers with their horses and traps awaiting customers; a small lad with a trolley; an invalid Bath chair; bicycles and prams; some well-dressed folk and a bare footed boy. The photograph is the work of local photographer Robert George Murduck who had studios in The Strand.

On the opposite page is an aerial photograph showing the Beacon, the Clock Tower and the Gentlemen's Club, now the Elizabeth Hall but a much smaller building.

Bicycles on the beach? Maybe the fore-runners of jet-skis. Note how all those pictured in this Edwardian scene (below) are so formally dressed, including the cyclists in their three-piece suits and caps. Even Holy Trinity church is "wearing" some scaffolding!

The local bicycle dealer in those days was S. Burrow with premises in Exeter Road. Sydney Burrow, in the centre, had the distinction of being the first person in Exmouth to have a

motor car and he also opened the town's first commercial garage.

The lifeboat always holds an attraction for visitors and those in Exmouth on September 1, 1954 had the added delight of witnessing the Naming Ceremony of a new boat. The *Maria Noble* was named by Air Vice Marshall H. V. Satterley at a ceremony combined with one at which the Exmouth Lifeboat Station was presented with a 150th Anniversary Commemorative Vellum by Lady Peters. The photograph for this card was taken by Richard Tarr of Exmouth.

A sea-water bath house in Victorian times and the Harbour Cafe in more recent years, this sea-front building was the headquarters of Exmouth Yacht Club when this card card was sent in 1911.

A suitable subject for a postcard was a person who was considered to be something of a 'character', and a man in his 80s noted for producing ingenious figures and scenes in sand certainly fell within that category. Local photographer W. A. Puddicombe took this picture of the Exmouth beach sand artist with his creation of Lady Godiva.

"We like Exmouth very much" ... So began the message on this card sent home to Bristol by a holidaymaker in 1917. And to emphasise the point, the writer went on ... "We drove to Budleigh Salterton on Friday. We did not care much for it and are glad we are here instead."

Can't come home, am engaged
at EXMOUTH.

AGNES · RICHARDSON·

(Above) Churches were popular subjects for postcards in days gone by. The Parade Methodist Church, situated as its name implies on The Parade, was demolished in 1966 to make way for a supermarket which, in later years, has become a clothing store.

(Opposite) In stark contrast to the picture above, these characters with a twinkle in their eyes front a card whose message began, "Dear Mary, Don't you think you ought to come down and take care of us? I don't say I do this every night ..."

Here we have two contrasting examples of the humour conveyed by comic holiday postcards in days gone by. A 1920s "Pocket Novelty Card" with a flap which lifts up to reveal a dozen small photographs of Exmouth. Although this one was posted with a 1d stamp, the postcard rate, the recipient had to pay an extra 1d as being "liable to letter rate".

The Devon Porker

You may push me
You may shuv
But I'm hanged
If I'll be druv
From EXMOUTH.

This little Devon Porker is intent in remaining in Exmouth and conveys his feelings with a dose of good old Devon dialect!

P2657. Exmouth from the Air

This is another aerial view card in which may be seen Chapel Street in its pre-Magnolia Centre days, the Montague Burton tailor's shop prominent in The Parade is also visible just above the line "Exmouth from the Air". The old railway station can just be seen at the bottom just right of centre but the

railway lines are out of view. The line of Rolle Street runs diagonally to the top left from The Strand as Holy Trinity Church becomes an obvious landmark. The Esplanade can be spied along the top of picture with the clock tower and lifeboat station as identifiable features.

A day out on a "charabanc" was as much appreciated by residents as holiday-makers. And what better souvenir of that enjoyable event than a postcard. The bottom photograph shows a mixed group about to depart from outside All Saints Church, while the other was taken at the start of a local Conservative Women's Section outing.

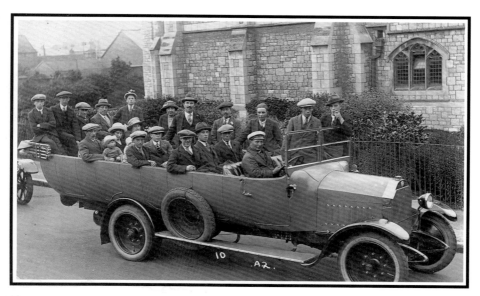

"X marks the spot." It was the practice of some visitors to try and find a picture postcard showing his or her hotel or boarding house and mark it with a cross to give those back home some idea of the holiday residence. Which is just what one lady did in July 1916.

Esplanade and Morton Crescent, Exmouth   JV 58258

The former pavilion which stood on the nearby Exmouth Pier was used for a variety of purposes during its lifetime and in 1909 the attraction was skating. The small building adjoining the pavilion bears a sign "A.A. Chown, Practical Tailor and Outfitter."

A visitor, 'enchanted' with Exmouth, was the sender of a card showing Maer Beach in 1926, although she wasn't too happy about the journey to Devon. Her message was: "We arrived yesterday evening at 6.30 and had had about enough of trains for one day. This looks to be a lovely place and we have very comfortable rooms. Having a morning on the beach in a deck chair."

Postmarked August 1934, this picture of the Sands must have been one of the first to feature the newly-opened Pavilion which can be seen in the distance. The card is a "Real Photo", one by the noted Dawlish postcard producers, Chapman & Son.

CHRIS WEEDE AND HIS "CRAZY FARE"

Concert parties were a major seaside attraction in days gone by and a postcard of a favourite show was a 'must' for the holidaymaker, either to send home or to keep as a souvenir. The Aristocrats are pictured below during their 1924 Exmouth season while the Chris Weede and his Crazy Fare card was even autographed by Chris Weede himself!

"This is where I bought a swim-suit." The drapery shop of James Pulsford & Son occupied the important corner shop at the junction of Exeter Road and The Parade for the first thirty years or so of this century. Those were the days when people could amble along in the roadway without any fear of being knocked down or run over.

New Year Greetings for 1909 were conveyed by this view of residential properties in the upper part of Albion Street. The absence of vehicles is practically the only difference from the same scene today.

Rolle Street has been a popular area for shopping since 1868 when Messrs Clapp's & Messrs Chowns opened their first shops there. In Edwardian times the horse and carriage was a familiar sight.

A special postcard to commemorate a special occasion. Photographer Robert George Murduck produced such a card in 1911 as a souvenir of an open-air public meal in Phear Park to celebrate the Coronation of King George V and Queen Mary. The park had been given to the people of Exmouth by members of the Phear family, for use as a public open space, just a couple of years earlier.

Having close and strong associations with the sea and ships, it was inevitable that a Seamen's Mission and Sailors' Rest should be established in Exmouth. After occupying premises first near the Docks and then on Chapel Hill, a purpose built property was erected, thanks to public subscriptions, in St Andrew's Road. This card, showing the new building, was sent shortly after it opened in 1909.

Soon the motor car began to make its appearance but in the 1930s it was still possible to park without trouble anywhere along The Parade and visit Woolworth's, when it was still the "3d and 6d Stores".

Park Road used to be a deserted road in which a couple of men could stand and enjoy a chat. This 1922 card shows the bridge carrying the Exmouth–Budleigh Salterton railway line across the top of the road.

There used to be a choice of refreshment on Chapel Hill – a drink in W. J. Axon's Pilot Inn or a ham and beef tea in M & W Westcott's Restaurant. The Pilot Inn has changed little over the years, but the adjoining restaurant was demolished in 1939. The new building on the site was a newspaper office and then an estate agent's before turning full circle and becoming a restaurant again.

P. 2661. Exmouth from the Air.

The Harbour, Exmouth

(Above) Channel View was a popular seafront hotel in the 1930s. The building – with some alterations – still stands, but now serves the holidaymaker in a variety of other ways. Standing next to the Deer Leap, it is a familiar building to locals, but did you recognise it?

(Opposite Top) For many years there was a round-the-year ferry service across the Exe Estuary. Now it operates only during the summer months. Although this card is entitled Exmouth Starcross Ferry, the ferry boat is almost hidden by the Salcombe-registered *Marie* and two Exeter-based vessels *Melita* and *Prince*.

(Opposite Bottom) Until its recent closure, Exmouth Docks was a hive of activity and a special attraction for holidaymakers was to watch the cargo vessels come and go. The dock basin was home for large and small vessels alike and until the 1960s, a railway line ran from the station to the Dockside. Besides highlighting the Docks basin, the aerial view shows other buildings which have now disappeared such as the Pier with its Pavilion; the Shelly road colony of small chalets and holiday homes; dockside works buildings; and the slipway cafe.

Until just before the First World War, the Queen's Drive running along the sea front to Orcombe Point was just a footpath, popular for family walks, pushing a pram or riding a tricycle. This card, posted on September 16, 1908 only bore the name and address of the recipient in Leicester. There was no message nor any indication as to the sender. Maybe the sender and addressee were not on speaking terms!

"Big oaks from little acorns grow." With the passing of the years, a few huts and tents in a rural setting became the popular Sandy Bay holiday complex of today.

Withycombe, as a village in its own right, was mentioned in the Domesday Book (1086). The Holly Tree Inn – Stocker's Holly Tree Inn as the notice in this picture states – dates back to Victorian times. It still remains, but most of the other buildings have altered since this card was sent in 1911.

A delightful rural scene, at Littleham, but this card sent in 1943 carried a rather sombre and sobering message: "Where Uncle Joe is buried and where one day I shall have to follow. You can see a little bit of the graveyard." At least Uncle Joe was in good company as the Littleham graveyard was also the last resting place of Lady Nelson, the wife of naval hero Lord Horatio Nelson.

The manufacturers of Pears Soap and Holloway's Pills and Ointments made sure that holidaymakers in Edwardian times were aware of their products by advertising on bathing machines. A holidaymaker with a sense of humour wrote on this card "Just a card to let you see where I am having my treatment! The Bathing Machine in the picture is the place! Am taking the waters, massage etc!! My address until further notice – c/o Holloways Pills & Ointment Bathing Machine, The Sands, Exmouth."

"Isn't this a nice station?" asked the sender of this card in 1929. Exmouth has had a station since the railway came to the town in May 1861 but this attractive red-brick building, designed by Sir William Tite, was opened in 1926. It was demolished forty four years later and replaced by the present, smaller single-storeyed station eighty yards further from Imperial Road. And that, my friends, is the end of the line for us too ...